The Way of the Sunlit Path

Acknowledgements

All quoted texts are the copyright of their respective writers and publishers. The significances given under the flower photos are from "Flower and their messages" by the Mother (Sri Aurobindo Ashram Press, 2012)

The Way of the Sunlit Path
Copyright : Prisma, Auroville

Second revised edition 2023

ISBN 978-93-95460-92-7 (Paperpack)
ISBN 978-93-95460-89-7 (ebook)

BISAC Code:
OCC000000, BODY, MIND & SPIRIT / General
HEA025000,m HEALTH & FITNESS / Yoga
PHI015000, PHILOSOPHY / Mind & Body
JNF040000, JUVENILE NONFICTION / Philosophy
HEA025000, HEALTH & FITNESS / Yoga

Thema Subject Category:
JBCC9, History of ideas
Q, Philosophy and Religion
QRA, Religion: general

Cataloging-in-Publication Data for this title is available from the Library of Congress.

Published by:
PRISMA, an imprint of Digital Media Initiatives
PRISMA, Aurelec/ Prayogshala,
Auroville 605101, Tamil Nadu, India
www.prisma.haus

Contents

Foreword	1
The Origin and Context of the Sunlit Path	3
Mother	8
Sri Aurobindo	11
Nolini Kant Gupta	32
Satprem	35
Morwenna Donnelly	45
Alain Grandcolas	55
Maggi Lidchi Grassi	58
Nolini Kanta Gupta	59
Nagin Doshi	62
Narendra Thakkar	65
Vikas (Alan Vickers)	65
Narad	66
Kireet Joshi	67
Rosemary Meran	70
"... The Happy Sunlit Path"	73
Epilogue	75

Foreword

The Way of the Sunlit Path is an annotated research about a neglected and even misunderstood energy in the Integral Yoga of Sri Aurobindo and the Mother.

The intention is to understand this key perspective in a way that will direct our life journey toward the Mind of Light. The benefit of having all these original references together is invaluable for our awakening in the new consciousness that Integral Yoga represents. Since these quotations are dispersed throughout the writings of Sri Aurobindo and Mother, we might miss their significance among the expansive revelations that Integral Yoga offers us.

Franz and B (long-term residents of Auroville, India) have talked about the "Sunlit Path" for years and finally organized the references together. The contextual and personal commentary is to highlight and clarify this sunlit way as much as we can. We have quoted a few scholars and poets to elucidate this Sunlit Path beyond the source references.

May The Way of the Sunlit Path be a convenient guide for activating this ancient truth as a support for conscious evolution. May it illumine the transformation offered to us in Integral Yoga.

20 November 2020

Perfect path
For each one it is the path that leads fastest to the Divine.
Coffea.

The Origin and Context of the Sunlit Path

In the ancient Vedic heritage of India, dating back more than ten thousand years, a link is found within these oral traditions to a sunlit path toward higher realizations. The evocative metaphor of a "sunlit path" is timeless and appealing. Most important, it is a truth, a universal truth. Human beings naturally seek the light until conditioned to do otherwise. Each person's human nature is shaped by a nurturing which is very seldom enlightened about our true nature as embodied spirits. Then when fear dominates love, the soul loses its connection to its Source.

Throughout human history, most cultures have used forms of fear for control. Within religious and spiritual practices this has been the norm. We can also identify the mental polarity that splits the spiritual and the material into separate realities. That error persists even today in spite of the advances in sciences like quantum physics which prove otherwise. Also persisting in the spirit/matter split is the lack of an accommodation for Oneness. The logical paradox of "the one and the many" co-existing must resolve itself with a unified consciousness.

Knowledge, personal and cosmic, divided into different approaches will block progress if it falls into the limitations of disjunctive thought, of judgmental thought, as in good/bad, right/wrong, true/false, which become imprisoning perceptions through exclusion, The universal embrace of the so-called negative, shadow, or catastrophic must be there as well. "Spiritual" paths are especially vulnerable to divisive and contradictory ideologies due to our mental limitations. So it happened with the sunlit path versus the way of struggle and suffering. Most often the stress is on the need for a suffering path to overcome the obstacles blocking a spiritual life. The ascetic model still popularly prevails for spiritual progress: "no pain, no gain."

Generally speaking, the traditions of religions come with a gravity that human nature does not enthusiastically embrace. Sri Aurobindo's insight that "all life is yoga" is not commonly understood. Most do not realize that we are doing "yoga" just by being incarnated and all our activity is conscious or unconscious. A realization that we are by nature spiritual beings in a real sense more than we are merely mortal, is not practically grasped. Gripped in the trance of material existence and survival, most are trapped by it until there is some sort of awakening. When the adventure of consciousness begins, the door of "yoga" or connection opens. Then the Integral Yoga of Sri Aurobindo and the Mother is possible. This yoga is based on the evolution of the human being to a more conscious state and the leap to a new species. In this radical approach, we find an open and universal process without religion or dogmatic teachings. In fact, the Mother declared that their yoga is not even a teaching, but "an action upon earth." Sri Aurobindo articulated with clarity his work and mission extensively in his collection of written works, while the Mother, beside the collections of her talks, classes, and messages, gave us the gift of a personal agenda describing her experiences in depth. The Integral Yoga now also has a library of compilations and commentaries on this Yoga that grows continuously.

How then do we account for the anomaly that a core revelation in this Yoga, emphasized by both Mother and Sri Aurobindo, has received so little attention? Why is it often misunderstood even within the community of those associated with this Integral Yoga? Humanity at this stage of evolution still tends to believe there is an inner psychological suffering between the shadow and the light. The dark and the negative are most often assumed to have the advantage, at least in the short term. Heroics seem to be called for to overcome the obstacles to living in the light. Resistances to the light seem to require conquering warriors according to most approaches. Such perspectives may seriously distort the spiritual journey and be counter-productive, or even disastrous. Some more recent theologies and psychologies have exposed the flaws in this understanding, but they have not impacted enough to change or replace this mindset. The Mother had an "ambition" to change this mindset:

After much study and observation, I have a sort of "spiritual ambition" (if it can be called that) to bring to the world a sunlit path to eliminate the necessity for struggle and suffering.
　　　　　　　　The Mother, Agenda, Vol. 2, p. 260 (30.9.1961).

B first learned about the sunlit path from Morweena Donnelly, an Irish professor at Cambridge University who wrote: *Founding the Life Divine; an Introduction to the Integral Yoga of Sri Aurobindo*. She influenced Edith Schnapper another professor who wrote the *The Spiral Path*. Edith became a founder together with Joy Calvert of Auroville International UK. Morweena commissioned a large stained-glass window that combines the symbols of Sri Aurobindo and the Mother to be placed the center they started together. Later, Joy and Edith preserved this window for decades until it found a final home in the Solar Kitchen of Auroville. In the center of the dining room, facing east toward the sun, this many-splendored window greets the hundreds who daily come for lunch. That window reminds us about the sunlit path. B read Morweena's book before he came to Auroville and was touched with what he thought was a progressive revelation from Sri Aurobindo that she had highlighted. When he came to Auroville in the early seventies, he was dismayed to find hardly anyone had any clear understanding about the sunlit path. He never found that any of the commentators on Integral Yoga in their writings or talks ever said more than a passing remark about such a path. Many are familiar with the phrase "sunlit path," but if you go deeper, very few seem to know what it means, and worse, there can be a wrong or dismissive view. B recently heard it called a Pollyana perspective. Fake news for sure. Even in the original Pollyana novel and in the Walt Disney movie version, as so well-played by Haley Mills, she is more of a perceptive realist who knew the power of positive thought, than a scatter-brained romantic looking at the world through rose-colored glasses. Pollyana walked the sunlit path but popular culture demeaned her as a symbol of naive optimism because it is only slowly dawning on us how much our thinking actually determines our reality.

The Sri Aurobindo Ashram has continued to publish over the years a popular compilation titled *The Sunlit Path*. That booklet does lay out enlightening quotations from the Mother but omits to mention anything about what she has said directly about this path. Perhaps only Satprem, the French writer who compiled his extensive conversations with Mother (*The Mother's Agenda* of thirteen volumes) seemed to really grasp the significance of this path. Mother directly addressed both his negativity about it, and commended what he later wrote about the sunlit path. Most

people cannot grasp that suffering is optional. Mother, however, insisted on it personally to Satprem:
... *you don't need to suffer; it's not necessary.*
That's what I want to tell you.
Mother's Agenda, Vol. II, p. 36

When Satprem read the third chapter of his book Supermanhood titled: "The Sunlit Path," The Mother remained looking at him for a long time. And then smiling said:
You've entered a new world.... For those who can follow you, it will be good!
Oh, it's quite new.... (Smiling and approving) It's extraordinary, you understand, it's ...
The impression that a new door has opened. The impression as if you had opened a new door for humanity.
You're the one who opens it!
Mother's Agenda Vol. 11 17 October 1970

What I call "being on the path" is being in a state of consciousness in which only union with the Divine has any value - this union is the only thing worth living, the sale object of aspiration. Everything else has lost all value and is not worth seeking, so there is no longer any question of renouncing it because it is no longer an object of desire.

As long as union with the Divine is not the thing for which one lives, one is not yet on the path.

The Mother

Mother

The path is long but self-surrender makes it short; the path is difficult but perfect trust makes it easy. . . .

There are two paths of Yoga, one of tapasya (discipline), and the other of surrender. The path of tapasya is arduous. Here you rely solely upon yourself, you proceed by your own strength. You ascend and achieve according to the measure of your force. There is always the danger of falling down. And once you fall, you lie broken in the abyss and there is hardly a remedy. The other path, the path of surrender, is safe and sure. It is here, however, that the Western people find their difficulty. They have been taught to fear and avoid all that threatens their personal independence. They have imbibed with their mothers' milk the sense of individuality. And surrender means giving up all that. In other words, you may follow, as Ramakrishna says, either the path of the baby monkey or that of the baby cat. The baby monkey holds to its mother in order to be carried about and it must hold firm, otherwise if it loses its grip, it falls. On the other hand, the baby cat does not hold to its mother, but is held by the mother and has no fear nor responsibility; it has nothing to do but to let the mother hold it and cry ma ma. If you take up this path of surrender fully and sincerely, there is no more danger or serious difficulty. The question is to be sincere. If you are not sincere, do not begin Yoga. If you were dealing in human affairs, then you could resort to deception; but in dealing with the Divine there is no possibility of deception anywhere. You can go on the Path safely when you are candid and open to the core and when your only end is to realise and attain the Divine and to be moved by the Divine.

Consciousness turned towards the Light
It thirsts for the light and cannot live without it.
Helianthus. Sunflower

To the students:

Sri Aurobindo has written in Savitri:

*"Yes, there are happy ways near to God's sun;
But few are they who tread the sunlit path;
Only the pure in soul can walk in light."*

*What a joy it would be to possess the required purity!
When one is living among men with all their miseries, it is only the
Grace that can bestow this state - even in those who by Tapasya
have abolished their ego.
It is beyond all personal effort*
7 May 1968 Questions and Answers

Mother's "vision" of the Sunlit Path

*All was gold and gold and gold,
a torrent of golden light pouring down in an uninterrupted flow
and bringing with it the consciousness that the path of the gods
is a Sunlit Path in which difficulties lose all reality.
Such is the path open before us if we choose to take it.*
Words of the Mother, vol II, p 31

SRI AUROBINDO

It is in his *Letters on Yoga* that Sri Aurobindo answered the questions and doubts of disciples and devotees about the sunlit path:

Peace was the very first thing that the Yogins and seekers of old asked for, and it was a quiet and silent mind — and that always brings peace — that they declared to be the best condition for realizing the Divine. A cheerful and Sunlit heart is the fit vessel for the Ananda, and who shall say that Ananda or what prepares it is an obstacle to the Divine union? As for despondency, it is surely a terrible burden to carry on the way...

I know perfectly well that pain and suffering and struggle and excesses of despair are natural — though not inevitable — on the way, — not because they are helps, but because they are imposed on us by the darkness of this human nature out of which we have to struggle into the Light. I do not suppose Ramakrishna or Vivekananda would have recommended the incidents you allude to as an example for others to follow — they would surely have said that faith, fortitude, perseverance were the better way. That after all was what they stuck to in the end in spite of these bad moments, and they would never have dreamed of giving up the Yoga or the aspiration for the Divine on the ground that they were unfit and not meant for the realization.

.... I myself insist on the realization in this life and not after six or a lakh of births more. But the point of these stories [Ramakrishna's parable of Narada's story of the ascetic versus the bhakta] is in the moral and surely when Ramakrishna told it, he was not ignorant that there was a Sunlit Path of Yoga! He even seems to say that it is the quicker way as well as the better! You are quite mistaken in thinking that the possibility of the Sunlit Path is a discovery or original invention of mine. The very first books on Yoga I read more than thirty years ago spoke of the dark and Sunlit Way and emphasized the superiority of the second over the other.

It is not either because I have myself trod the Sunlit Way or flinched from difficulty and suffering and danger. I have had my full share of these things and the Mother has had ten times her full share. But that was because the finders of the Way had to face these things in order to conquer. No difficulty that can come on the sadhak but has faced us on the path; against many we have had to struggle hundreds of times (in fact that is an understatement) before we could overcome; many still remain protesting that they have a right until the perfect perfection is there. But we have never consented to admit their inevitable necessity for others. It is in fact to ensure an easier path to others hereafter that we have borne that burden. It was with that object that the Mother once prayed to the Divine that whatever difficulties, dangers, sufferings were necessary for the path might be laid on her rather than on others. It has been so far heard that as a result of daily and terrible struggles for years those who put an entire and sincere confidence in her are able to follow the Sunlit Path and even those who cannot, yet when they do put the trust find their path suddenly easy and, if it becomes difficult again, it is only when distrust, revolt, abhiman, or other darknesses come upon them. The Sunlit Path is not altogether a fable.

But you will ask what of those who cannot? Well, it is for them I am putting forth all my efforts to bring down the supramental Force within a measurable time. I know that it will descend but I am seeking its near descent and, with whatever dark obstruction of the earth-nature or furious inroads of the Asuric forces seeking to prevent it, it is approaching the terrestrial soil. The supramental is not, as you imagine, something cold, hard and rocklike. It bears within it the presence of the Divine Love as well as the Divine Truth and its reign here means for those who accept it the straight and thorn-less path on which there is no wall or obstacle of which the ancient Rishis saw the far-off promise.

The dark path is there and there are many who make like the Christians a gospel of spiritual suffering; many hold it to be the unavoidable price of victory. It may be so under certain circumstances, as it has been in so many lives at least at the beginning, or one may choose to make it so. But then the price has to be paid with resignation, fortitude or a tenacious resilience. I admit that if borne in that way the attacks of the Dark Forces or the ordeals they impose have a meaning. After each victory gained over them, there is then a sensible advance; often they seem to show us the difficulties in ourselves which we have to overcome and to say, "Here you must conquer us and here." But all the same it is a too dark and difficult way which nobody should follow on whom the necessity does not lie.[1]

There is nothing spiritually wrong in being glad and cheerful, on the contrary it is the right thing. As for struggles and aspiration, struggles are really not indispensable to progress and there are many people who get so habituated to the struggling attitude that they have all the time struggles and very little else.

---

1 Letters on Yoga—II, Bhakti Yoga and Vaishnavism, pp. 469-473

That is not desirable. There is a Sunlit Path as well as a gloomy one and it is the better of the two—a path in which one goes forward in absolute reliance on the Mother, fearing nothing, sorrowing over nothing. Aspiration is needed but there can be a Sunlit Aspiration full of light and faith and confidence and joy. If difficulty comes, even that can be faced with a smile.[2]

A true key for the Faery Palace.

The light which you saw seems to have got clouded by your indulging your vital more and more in the bitter pastime of sadness. That was quite natural, for that is the result sadness always does bring. It is the reason why I object to the gospel of sorrow and to any sadhana which makes sorrow one of its main planks (abhimān, revolt, viraha). For sorrow is not, as Spinoza pointed out, a passage to a greater perfection, a way to siddhi; it cannot be, for it confuses and weakens and distracts the mind, depresses the vital force, darkens the spirit. A relapse from joy and vital elasticity and Ananda to sorrow, self-distrust, despondency and weakness is a recoil from a greater to a lesser consciousness; — the habit of these moods shows a clinging of something in the vital to the smaller, obscurer, dark and distressed movement out of which it is the very aim of Yoga to rise.

It is incorrect to say that the wrong key with which you were trying to open the faery palace has been taken away from you and you are left with none at all. The true key has been given to you in the right kind or condition of meditation — a state

---

2 Letters on Yoga IV, Cheerfulness and Happiness, p. 175

Road to the Divine
Always long, apparently dry at times,
but always abundant in its results. *Drimiopsis kirkii*.

of inner rest, not of straining, of quiet opening, not of eager or desperate pulling, a harmonious giving of oneself to the Divine Force for its working, and in that quietude a sense of the Force working and a restful confidence allowing it to act without any unquiet interference. Now that condition is the beginning of the psychic opening; there is of course much more that afterwards comes to complete it but this is the fundamental condition into which all the rest can most easily come. In this condition there may and will be call, prayer, aspiration. Intensity, concentration will come of themselves, not by a hard effort or tense strain on the nature. Rejection of wrong movements, frank confession of defects are not only not incompatible, but helpful to it; but this attitude makes the rejection, the confession easy, spontaneous, entirely complete and sincere and effective. That is the experience of all who have consented to take this attitude. Now as to the tension and stiffness. I may say in passing that consciousness and receptivity are not the same thing; one may be receptive, yet externally unaware of how things are being done and of what is being done. But for such an external unconsciousness there must be a reason, — and in you it was the stiffness created by a tension and a straining which made the consciousness thus rigid and closed it up. Not that it closed you to the Force or that it took away the inner receptivity, but it did close you to the surface consciousness of what is being done. When that happens, the Force works, as I have repeatedly written, behind the veil; the results remain packed behind and come out afterwards, often slowly, little by little, until there is so much pressure that it breaks through somehow and forces open the external nature. There lies the difference between a mental and vital straining and pulling and a spontaneous psychic openness, and it is not at all the first time that we have spoken of the difference. It is not really a question of the right or the wrong key, but of putting the key in the lock in the right or the wrong way, whether because of some difficulty you try to force the lock turning the key this way and that with violence or confidently and quietly give it the right turn — and the door opens.

It is not that this pulling and straining and tension can do nothing; in the end they prevail for some result or another, but with difficulty, delay, struggle, strong upheavals of the Force breaking through in spite of all. Ramakrishna himself began by pulling and straining and got his result but at the cost of a tremendous and perilous upsetting; afterwards he took the quiet psychic way whenever he wanted a result and got it with ease and in a minimum time. You say that this way is too difficult for you but it is on the contrary the easiest and simplest and most direct way and anyone can do it, if he makes his mind and vital quiet. It is the other way of tension and strain and hard endeavour that is difficult and needs a great force of Tapasya. Take the psychic attitude; follow the straight Sunlit Path, with the Divine openly or secretly upbearing you — if secretly, he will yet show himself in good time, — do not insist on the hard, hampered, roundabout and difficult journey.

All this has been pointed out before: but you were not inclined to regard it as feasible or at least not ready to apply it in the field of meditation because your consciousness by tradition, owing to past lives and for other reasons, was clinging to former contrary conceptions. Something in you was harking back to one kind of Vaishnava sadhana, and that tended to bring in it its pain-giving feeling-elements of abhimāna, revolt, suffering, the Divine hiding himself ("always I seek, but never does he show himself") — the rarity of the unfolding and the milana.

Something else in you was inclined to see as the only alternative some harsh, grim ascetic ideal, the blank featureless Brahman (and imagined that the supramental was that), something in the vital looked on the conquest of wrong movements as a hard desperate tapasya, not as a passage into the purity and joy of the Divine — even now some element in you seems to insist on regarding the psychic attitude as something extraordinary, difficult, inhuman and impossible! There were these and other old lingerings of the mind and the vital; you have to clear them out and look at the simplicity of the Truth with a straight and simple gaze.

The remedy we propose, the key we offer to you ought not to be so difficult to apply as you imagine. After all, it is only applying in "meditation" the way that has been so successful with you in your creative work. There is a way of creation by strain and tension, by beating of the brain, by hard and painful labour — often the passage clogged and nothing coming or else coming only in return for a sort of intellectual tapasya. There is the other way in which one remains quiet and opens oneself to a power that is there behind and waits for inspiration; the force pours in and with it the inspiration, the illumination, the Ananda, — all is done by an inner Power. The flood passes, but one remains quiet for the next flood and at its time surely it comes. Here too all is not perfect at once; but progress comes by ever new waves of the same Power. Not then a strain of mental activity, but a restful opening to the Force that is there all the time above and around you, so that it may flow freely and do its work in peace and illumination and Ananda. The way has been shown to you, you yourself have had from time to time the true condition; only you must learn how to continue in it or recover it and you must allow the Force to do its work in its own way. It may take some time to take entire hold of it, get the other habit out and make this normal; but you must not start by deciding that it is impossible! It is eminently possible and it is the door of definitive entrance. The difficulty, the struggle were only the period of preparation necessary to get rid of or to exhaust the obstruction in the consciousness which was a thorn-hedge round the faery palace.[3]

If the ego is gone and the full surrender is there, then there should be no obstacles [to following the Sunlit Path of sadhana]. If however the rajas of the vital is only quiescent, then its quiescence may bring up the tamas in its place, and that would be the obstacle.[4]

The Sunlit Path can only be followed if the psychic is constantly or usually in front or if one has a natural spirit of faith and surrender or a face turned habitually towards the sun or psychic predisposition (e.g. a faith in one's spiritual destiny) or if he has acquired the psychic turn. That does not mean that the Sunlit Man has no difficulties; he may have many, but he regards them cheerfully as "all in the day's work". If he gets bad beatings, he is capable of saying, "Well, that was a queer go, but the Divine is evidently in a queer mood and if that is his way of doing things, it must be the right one; I am surely a still queerer fellow myself and that, I suppose, was the only means of putting me right." But everybody can't be of that turn, and surrender which would put everything right is, as you say, difficult to do

---

3 Letters on Yoga—IV, Chapter III, Depression and Despondency, pp.190-193
4 Letters on Yoga—IV, Ego and Its Forms, pp. 233

completely. That is why we do not insist on total surrender at once, but are satisfied with a little to begin with, the rest to grow as it can.

I have explained to you why so many people (not by any means all) are in this gloomy condition, dull and despondent. It is the tamas, the inertia of the Inconscient, that has got hold of them. But also it is the small physical vital which takes only an interest in the small and trivial things of the ordinary daily and social life and nothing else. When formerly the sadhana was going on on higher levels (mind, higher vital etc.), there was plenty of vigour and verve and interest in the details of the Ashram work and life as well as in an inner life; the physical vital was carried in the stream. But for many this has dropped; they live in the unsatisfied vital physical and find everything desperately dull, gloomy and without interest or issue. In their inner life the tamas from the Inconscient has created a block or a bottleneck and they do not find any way out. If one can keep the right condition and attitude, a strong interest in work or a strong interest in sadhana, then this becomes quiescent. That is the malady. Its remedy is to keep the right condition and to bring gradually or, if one can, swiftly the light of the higher aspiration into this part of the being also, so that whatever the conditions of the environment, it may keep also the right poise. Then the Sunlit Path should be less impossible.[5]

I don't believe much in this Divine Darkness. It is a Christian idea. For us the Divine is Peace, Purity, Wideness, Light, Ananda.[6]

---

5 Letters on Yoga—IV, The Inconscient and the Integral Yoga, p.618
6 Letters on Yoga—IV, The Right Attitude towards Difficulties, p. 681

Hope
Paves life's way.
Jacquemontia pentantha.

Resolving Contradictory Impressions

There is no contradiction between my former statements about the Sunlit Path and what I have said about the difficult and unpleasant passages which the Yoga has to pass through in its normal development in the way of human nature. The Sunlit Path can be followed by those who are able to practice surrender, first a central surrender and afterwards a more complete self-giving in all the parts of the being. If they can achieve and preserve the attitude of the central surrender, if they can rely wholly on the Divine and accept cheerfully whatever comes to them from the Divine, then their path becomes Sunlit and may even be straightforward and easy. They will not escape all difficulties, no seeker can, but they will be able to meet them without pain and despondency, — as indeed the Gita recommends that Yoga should be practiced, anirvin. n. acetasā , — trusting in the inner guidance and perceiving it more and more or else in the outer guidance of the Guru. It can also be followed even when one feels no light and no guidance if there is or if one can acquire a bright settled faith and happy bhakti or has the nature of the spiritual optimist and the firm belief or feeling that all that is done by the Divine is done for the best even when we cannot understand his action. But all have not this nature, most are very far from it, and the complete or even the central surrender is not easy to get and to keep it always is hard enough for our human nature. When these things are not there, the liberty of the soul is not attained and we have instead to undergo the law or fulfil a hard and difficult discipline.

Solutions to Break the Law of Ignorance

That law is imposed on us by the Ignorance which is the nature of all our parts; our physical being is obviously a mass of ignorance, the vital is full of ignorant desires and passions, the mind is also an instrument of Ignorance struggling towards some kind of imperfect and mostly inferior and external knowledge. The path of the seeker proceeds through this ignorance; for a long time he can find no light of solid experience or realization, only the hopes and ideas and beliefs of the mind which do not give the true spiritual seeing; or he gets glimpses of light or periods of light but the light often goes out and the luminous periods are followed by frequent or long periods of darkness. There are constant fluctuations, persistent disappointments, innumerable falls and failures. No path of Yoga is really easy or free from these difficulties or fluctuations; the way of bhakti is supposed to be the easiest, but still we find constant complaints that one is always seeking but never finding and even at the best there is a constant ebb and tide, milana and viraha, joy and weeping, ecstasy and despair. If one has the faith or in the absence of faith the will to go through, one passes on and enters into the joy and light of the divine realization. If one gets some habit of true surrender, then all this is not necessary; one can enter into the Sunlit Way. Or if one can get some touch of what is called pure bhakti, śuddhā bhakti, then whatever happens that is enough; the way becomes easy, or if it does not, still this is a sufficient start to support us to the end without the sufferings and falls that happen so often to the ignorant seeker.

The Necessity of Complete Transformation

In all Yoga there are three essential objects to be attained by the seeker: union or abiding contact with the Divine, liberation of the soul or the Self, the Spirit, and a certain change of the consciousness, the spiritual change. It is this change, which is necessary for reaching the other two objects, necessary at least to a certain degree, that is the cause of most of the struggles and difficulties; for it is not easy to accomplish it; a change of the mind, a change of the heart, a change of the habits of the will is called for and is obstinately resisted by our ignorant nature. In this Yoga a complete transformation of the nature is aimed at because that is necessary for the complete union and the complete liberation not only of the soul and the spirit but of the nature itself. It is also a Yoga of works and of the integral divine life; for that the integral transformation of nature is evidently necessary; the union with the Divine has to carry with it a full entrance into the divine consciousness and the divine nature; there must be not only sāyujya or sālokya but sādṛśya or, as it is called in the Gita, sā dharmya. The full Yoga, Purna Yoga, means a fourfold path, a Yoga of knowledge for the mind, a Yoga of bhakti for the heart, a Yoga of works for the will and a Yoga of perfection for the whole nature. But, ordinarily, if one can follow wholeheartedly any one of these lines, one arrives at the result of all the four. For instance, by bhakti one becomes close to the Divine, becomes intensely aware of Him and arrives at knowledge, for the Divine is the Truth and the Reality; by knowing Him, says the Upanishads, one comes to know all. By bhakti also the will is led into the road of the works of love and the service of the Divine and the government of the nature and its acts by the Divine, and that is Karmayoga. By bhakti also comes spiritual change of the consciousness and the action of the nature which is the first step towards its transformation. So it is with all the other lines of the fourfold path.

But it may be that there are many obstacles in the being to the domination of the mind and heart and will by bhakti and the consequent contact with the Divine. The too great activity of the intellectual mind and its attachment to its own pride of ideas, its prejudices, its fixed notions and its ignorant reason may shut the doors to the inner light and prevent the full tide of bhakti from flooding everything; it may also cling to a surface mental activity and refuse to go inside and allow the psychic vision and the feelings of the inner heart to become its guides, though it is by this vision and this feeling that bhakti grows and conquers. So too the passions and desires of the vital being and its ego may block the way and prevent the self-giving of the mind and heart to the Divine. The inertia, ignorance and inconscience of one's physical consciousness, its attachment to fixed habits of thought and feeling and action, its persistence in the old grooves may come badly in the way of the needed change. In such circumstances the Divine may have to bide his time; but if there is real hunger in the heart, all that cannot prevent the final realization; still, it may have to wait till the obstructions are removed or at least so much cleared out as to admit an unimpeded working of the Divine Power on the surface nature. Till then, there may be periods of inner ease and some light in the mind, periods also of the feeling of bhakti or of peace, periods of the joy of self-consecration in works and service; for these will take long to stay permanently and there will be much struggle and unrest and suffering. In the end the Divine's working will appear and one will be able to live in his presence.

Facing the Difficulties

I have described the difficulties of Yoga at their worst, as they may hamper and afflict even those predestined to the realization but as often there is an alternation or a mixture of the light and the darkness, initial attainment perhaps and heavy subsequent difficulties, progress and attacks and retardations, strong movements forward and a floundering in the bogs of the Ignorance. Even great realizations may come and high splendors of light and spiritual experience and yet the goal is not attained; for in the phrase of the Rig Veda, "As one climbs from peak to peak there is made clear the much that is still to be done." But there is always something that either carries us on or forces us on. This may take the shape of something conscious in front, the shape of a mastering spiritual idea, indestructible aspiration or fixed faith which may seem sometimes entirely veiled or even destroyed in periods of darkness or violent upheaval, but always they reappear when the storm has passed or the blackness of night has thinned, and reassert their influence. But also it may be something in the very essence of the being deeper than any idea or will in the mind, deeper and more permanent than the heart's aspiration but hidden from one's own observation. One who is moved to Yoga by some curiosity of the mind or even by its desire for knowledge can turn aside from the path from disappointment or any other cause; still more can those who take it up from some inner ambition or vital desire turn away through revolt or frustration or the despondency of frequent check and failure. But if this deeper thing is there, then one cannot permanently leave the path of spiritual endeavour: one may decide to leave the path but is not

allowed from within to do it or one may leave but is obliged to return to it by the secret spiritual need within him.

All these things are common to every path of Yoga; they are the normal difficulties, fluctuations and struggles which come across the path of spiritual effort. But in this Yoga there is an order or succession of the workings of the secret Force which may vary greatly in its circumstances in each sadhak, but still maintains its general line. Our evolution has brought the being up out of inconscient Matter into the Ignorance of mind, life and body tempered by an imperfect knowledge and is trying to lead us into the light of the Spirit, to lift us into that light and to bring the light down into us, into body and life as well as mind and heart and to fill with it all that we are. This and its consequences, of which the greatest is the union with the Divine and life in the divine consciousness, is the meaning of the integral transformation. Mind is our present topmost faculty; it is through the thinking mind and the heart with the soul, the psychic being behind them that we have to grow into the Spirit, for what the Force first tries to bring about is to fix the mind in the right central idea, faith or mental attitude and the right aspiration and poise of the heart and to make these sufficiently strong and firm to last in spite of other things in the mind and heart which are other than or in conflict with them. Along with this it brings whatever experiences, realizations or descent or growth of knowledge the mind of the individual is ready for at the time or as much of it, however small, as is necessary for its further progress: sometimes these realizations and experiences are very great and abundant, sometimes few and small or negligible; in some there seems to be in this first stage nothing much of these things or nothing decisive — the

Force seems to concentrate on a preparation of the mind only. In many cases the sadhana seems to begin and proceed with experiences in the vital; but in reality this can hardly take place without some mental preparation, even if it is nothing more than a turning of the mind or some kind of opening which makes the vital experiences possible. In any case, to begin with the vital is a hazardous affair; the difficulties there are more numerous and more violent than on the mental plane and the pitfalls are innumerable. The access to the soul, the psychic being, is less easy because it is covered up with a thick veil of ego, passion and desire. One is apt to be swallowed up in a maze of vital experiences, not always reliable, the temptation of small siddhis, the appeal of the powers of darkness to the ego. One has to struggle through these densities to the psychic being behind and bring it forward; then only can the sadhana on the vital plane be safe.

However that may be, the descent of the sadhana, of the action of the Force into the vital plane of our being becomes after some time necessary. The Force does not make a wholesale change of the mental being and nature, still less an integral transformation before it takes this step: if that could be done, the rest of the sadhana would be comparatively secure and easy. But the vital is there and always pressing on the mind and heart, disturbing and endangering the sadhana and it cannot be left to itself for too long. The ego and desires of the vital, its disturbances and upheavals have to be dealt with and if not at once expelled, at least dominated and prepared for a gradual if not a rapid modification, change, illumination . . .[7]

---

7   Letters on Yoga—IV, The Right Attitude towards Difficulties, pp. 685-691

Letter to Dilip Kumar Roy

I spoke of strange ideas in connection with what you said about peace and cheerfulness being obstacles in the Yoga because they are incompatible with an ardent longing for realisation. Peace was the very first thing that the Yogins and seekers of old asked for and it was a quiet and silent mind – and that always brings peace – that they declared to be the best condition for realising the Divine. A cheerful and Sunlit Heart is the fit vessel for the Ananda and who shall say that Ananda or what prepares it is an obstacle to the divine union? As for despondency, it is surely a terrible burden to carry on the way. One has to pass through it sometimes, like Christian of the Pilgrim's Progress through the Slough of Despond, but its constant reiteration cannot be anything but an obstacle. The Gita especially says, "Practise the Yoga with an undespondent heart, anirvinnacetasa.". . .

In any case one thing can never help and that is to despond always and say, "I am unfit; I am not meant for the Yoga". And worse still are these perilous mental formations such as you are always accepting that you must fare like Barin (one whose difficulty of exaggerated ambition was quite different from yours) and that you have only six years, etc. These are clear formations of the Dark Forces seeking not only to sterilise your aspiration but to lead you away and so prevent your sharing in the fruit of the victory hereafter. I do not know what Krishnaprem has said but his injunction, if you have rightly understood it, is one that cannot stand as valid, since so many have done Yoga relying on tapasya or anything else but not confident of any divine grace. It is not that, but the soul's demand for a higher truth or a higher life that is indispensable. Where that is, the Divine Grace whether believed in or not, will intervene. If you believe, that hastens and facilitates things; if you cannot yet believe, still the soul's aspiration will justify itself with whatever difficulty and struggle.

December 20, 1941,

In faith and confidence and joy on the quiet and sunlit path towards the home of Light and Ananda.

11. 2. 1936   Message for a disciple on her birthday

It is true that the path is very long, but for one who follows it with sincerity, it is really very interesting. . ..

The Mother

Nolini Kant Gupta

Sri Aurobindo speaks of the sunlit path in Yoga. It is the path of happy progress where dangers and difficulties, violent ups and downs are reduced to a minimum, if not altogether obviated. In ideal conditions it is as it were a smooth and fair-weather sailing, as much of course as it is humanly possible. What are then these conditions? It is when the sadhaka keeps touch with his inmost being, his psychic consciousness, when this inner Guide and Helmsman is given the charge; for then he will be able to pass sovereignly by all shoals and rocks and storm-racks, through all vicissitudes, gliding on—slow or swift as needed—Inevitably towards the goal. A doubting mind, an impetuous vital urge, an inert physical consciousness, though they may be there in any strength, cannot disturb or upset the even tenor of the forward march. Even outward circumstances bow down to the pressure of the psychic temperament and bring to it their happy collaboration.

This may not always mean that all is easy and difficulty is simply not, once the psychic is there. It becomes so when the psychic is there fully in front; even otherwise when the inner being is in the background, still sensed and, on the whole, obeyed, although there are battles, hard battles to be fought and won, then even a little of this Consciousness saves from a great fear. For, then, in all circumstances, you will have found a secret joy and cheer and strength that buoy you up and carry you through.

Like the individual, nations too have their sunlit path and the path of the doldrum as well. So long as a nation keeps to the truth of its inner being, follows its natural line of development, remains faithful to its secret godhead, it will have chosen that good part which will bring it divine blessings and fulfilment. But sometimes a nation has the stupidity to deny its self, to run after an ignis fatuus, a māyāmrga, then grief and sorrow and frustration lie ahead. We are afraid India did take such a wrong step when she refused to see the great purpose behind the present war and tried to avoid contributing her mite to the evolutionary Force at work. On the other hand Britain in a moment of supreme crisis, that meant literally life or death, not only to herself or to other nations, but to humanity itself, had the good fortune to be led by the right Inspiration, the whole nation rose as one man and swore allegiance to the cause of humanity and the gods. That was how she was saved and that was how she acquired a new merit and a fresh lease of life. Unlike Britain, France bowed down and accepted what should not have been accepted and cut herself adrift from her inner life and truth, the result was five years of hell. Fortunately, the hell in the end proved to be a purgatory, but what a purgatory! For there were souls who were willing to pay the price and did pay it to the full cash and nett. So France has been given the chance again to turn round and take up the thread of her life where it snapped.

Once more another crisis seems to be looming before the nations, once more the choice has to be made and acted upon. In our weakness it is natural and easy to invoke God, to feel the presence of a higher Guidance, to trust in a heavenly light; but it is in our strength that we must know whose strength it is, and in whose strength it is that we conquer.

If the present war has any meaning, as we all declare it has, then we must never lose sight of that meaning. And our true victory will come only in the process of the realisation of that meaning. That is the sunlit path we refer to here which the nations have to follow in their mutual dealings. It is the path of the evolutionary call to which we say we have responded and to which we must remain loyal and faithful in thought, in speech and in deed. If we see dark and ominous clouds gathering round us, dangers and difficulties suddenly raising their heads, then we must look about and try honestly to find out whether we have not strayed away from the sunlit path.

Collected Works of Nolini Kant Gupta, Vol 3, Part 3, Sunlit Path

Satprem

"And perhaps the whole work of Sri Aurobindo and Mother is to have brought the world the possibility of a sunlit path on which suffering, pain and disaster are no longer necessary in order to progress." (p. 146 *The Way of Supermanhood*) Satprem continued to elaborate the way of the sunlit path as a moment by moment choice of the light over death, the darkness. The sunlit path leads to the supramental sun. The sunlit path does not deny hell, it doesn't go that route. If it is imposed on the pilgrim of the path, the hell becomes a "shortcut to heaven" as Sri Aurobindo tells us in Savitri. Satprem gives us more context in his chapter on the The Victory over Death:

The supreme sun is at the bottom of the supreme darkness. "Death" is the passage to immortality, the keeper of the great total Sun, the ultimate compulsion toward integral Truth. At that moment, whatever is incapable of summoning the Light, all the unpurified fragments of being are immediately snapped up by that NO, dissolved in it, frozen in its black ecstasy, because they are themselves a little spark of that NO, a little refusal of that great Refusal, a chip of tha formidable Rock.

And, as a result, we have the key to everything that creates death in life – our countless little deaths every minute. And we understand that this body, this ever so fragile and insignificant little body, which others reject as an old rag or a hindrance to the supreme frolicking of the liberated Spirit, is in fact the site of a supreme conquest and a supreme deliverance, and that the heaven of the Sun of Truth is carved out on earth and in our body every minute by our adherence to or refusal of the light, by our choice, minute by minute, between our self of light and our self of death.

The supramental being is one forever delivered from death and, through his deliverance, the earth will be delivered, compelled to her supreme Sun by her supreme darkness.

"There are two paths," Sri Aurobindo said, the path of effort and the Sunlit Path. The path of effort is well known, it is the one that has ruled all our mental life, because we strive toward something we do not have or believe we do not have. We are beings full of shortcomings, of painful gaps and voids to be filled, but that void never fills; no sooner does it fill than another one appears and drags us into its new pursuit. We are like an absence of something that never finds its presence, apart from rare flashes which soon fade and seem to leave an even greater void. We may say that we lack this or that or this, but we lack only one thing, and that is ourselves - it is an absence of self. For what is really ourselves is full, since it is: all else passes away, comes and goes, but is not. How could what is need anything else? . . .

But where then is that elusive self? ... To ask the question is to knock at the door of the next circle, it is to turn in on ourselves for the second time. And there we need not theorize on what that self is, but we need to go in search of it and to discover it experimentally. And as we said, the method must develop in life and matter, since we can very well withdraw to our room and shut out the racket of the world, shut out its desires, tensions and countless tentacles, we can keep it all at grip's length, and, within our little inner circle, discover maybe some flash of self, some ineffable transcendence, but the minute we open the door of our room and relax our grip, everything will crowd back on us, like the screen of seaweed

over the diver, and we will find ourselves as before, only a little more unable to endure that racket and that torrent of tiny voracities biding their time. It is not by the grip of our virtues or our exceptional meditations that we will pass through that screen, but by something else and in another way. For, in fact, the self we must find is not a super-self, it is something else altogether. We shall therefore take ourselves as we are and where we are, at our physical and quite humdrum level. . . .

We may be French or American, but that is really a question of history and passport, another artifice that links us to one machinery or another, as our brother in Calcutta or Rangoon paces the same boulevard with the same question, under a yellow, red or orange flag. . . . Who is I? Who is I? Where is I? Where am I?.

And that little second, so vain, so frivolous amid that huge rush, is the true key to the discovery, an all-powerful lever that does not look like much - but truth does not look like much, as we know: if it did, we would soon have wrung its neck to systematize it and yoke it to one more machine. It is light, it slips through our fingers. It is a breath that blows past and refreshes everything.

. . . this drop of something else, this sudden little cry for nothing seems to go on, as if it had settled in a secret creek of our being where it vibrates and vibrates, one drop adding to another without ever decomposing, ever getting lost, accumulating on and on as if we had there an infallible stock, a haven filling up, a battery charging up little by little with another intensity of force which is like a beginning of bein.

And we set out on the Sunlit Path.

We are no longer fully in the machine, although it still snatches us at times, but only to make us feel its crushing tension, its obscure wheeling in a nothing that enmeshes a nothing that enmeshes nothing - we have tasted another air, even if it does not put on airs; we can no longer stand this non-existence which bustles from one point to another, from one telephone to another, one appointment to another, which climbs up and down the perpetual machinery, and nothing ever happens except the same never-ending story with other faces, other names and other words, on this boulevard or that one - it has to exist! ... We want to remember, perpetually remember and not slip along the boulevards like a jellyfish remember what? We do not even know what we have to remember - certainly not ourselves or the machinery or anything that again meshes one thing with another - a pure recall that finally becomes like a call, a fire burning for nothing, a little vibration of being that follows us everywhere and pervades everything, fills everything, every step, every gesture and every second, stretching even behind us, as if we walked in a new expanse with that little man before us who goes on and on but is no longer totally there, who has already broken loose, who breathes another air, listens to another song, walks to another rhythm - and it is almost like an eternal rhythm, vast and so soft. Then suddenly he raises his head in the middle of that boulevard, lifts his head above that rush, and his gaze is so clear, so luminous, almost joyful, sparkling and wide, sunny, embracing everything in a flash, and so triumphant, so sure, crystalline: a sudden royalty. We are, it is!

We are on the Sunlit Path, as if carried by this small growing vibration of being.

And we had no need of silence or of a snug room, no need to drive away the tentacles of life - on the contrary, the more they grasp us and try to strangle us, the more deafened we are by all this racket of life, and the more it burns inside, the hotter it gets, the more we need to be that and only that, that vibrating something else without which we cannot live or breathe - to forget it even for a second is to fall into complete suffocation. We walk the Sunlit Path amid the darkness of the world - inside, outside, it is all the same, alone or amid the crowd we are safe for ever, nothing and nobody can take that from us! Everywhere we carry our secret royalty, we grope our way in another geography where secret havens loom up, unexpected fjords, continents of peace and glimpses of unknown seas that seem to bring us the echo of a larger existence. We have lost our habit to want or not to want, our straining to get this or that, our struggle to live, struggle to become and to know: we are carried by another rhythm that has its own spontaneous knowledge, its clear life, its unpredictable wills and its sudden efficacies. We step into another realm, we run another gaze over the world, still a somewhat blind gaze, somewhat ignorant, but a gaze that feels and is as if pregnant with a yet unborn reality, widened by a yet unformulated knowledge, a wonder that does not dare. Perhaps we are like that brother ape from not so long ago, who ran strange eyes over his forest, or like those who ran, climbed and hunted so well but did not know the clear little vibration, the odd wonder, the sudden halt that seemed to tear obscure clouds and extend far, far ahead, in a vibrating expanse of creative possibilities.

On the Way to Supermanhood, pp.33-42

Satprem replies to a reader who misunderstands the path to the supramental

[Sri Aurobindo's] *yoga is integral because, instead of confining the quest to the spiritual heights, he has told us repeatedly that our body too must participate and we must bring the Spiritual Truth down into our body and our life. The way of ascent and all the others, the other planes of consciousness, are part of an integral development—for those who have the time and the special capacities that are required. But it is no longer the time for those excursions, since everything can be found here—since, in fact, Sri Aurobindo and Mother opened the way HERE. Please recall Mother's statement: "Sri Aurobindo came to tell us: one need not leave the earth to find the Truth, one need not leave life to find one's soul, one need not abandon the world or have limited beliefs to enter into relation with the Divine. The Divine is everywhere, in everything, and if he is hidden, it is because we do not take the trouble to find him."* (Questions and Answers, 8.13.1958)

And again this: *"For many, spiritual life is meditation. As long as that nonsense is not uprooted from human consciousness, the supramental force will always find it very difficult not to be swallowed up in the obscurity of an uncomprehending human mind."* (Questions and Answers, 4.17.1957) *And if you know how to read Sri Aurobindo and Mother, you will see that they have completely described this road of here and the—On the Way to Supermanhood only puts an intentionally exclusive accent on the "here," because there is no time to lose, because everyone does not have the special capacities for making large-scale explorations, and finally because we are at the Hour of God—we are right there! It has come. Because there really is something different in the world since 1969.*

It is not a change in Sri Aurobindo's yoga, it is the flowering of Sri Aurobindo's yoga, I dare say. I do not think that the flower of the flame tree contradicts in any way the flame tree.

Now, you have completely confused the psychic and the spiritual. The psychic, the soul, the Fire within, Agni, does not belong to the "mental bubble" or to any bubble: it is the Divine in matter. It is that little Fire which opens the door to the great solar Fire of the New Consciousness. It is the instrument of the yoga of the superman (when I speak of turning on the "psychic switch," I am there taking the word in the vulgar and ridiculous sense of people seeking visionary and occult experiences—not in the true sense). Others in every age have had the experience of the psychic, of the inner Fire, but aside from the Rishis, no one used it to transform matter; the religions have made a purely devotional and "mystical" thing out of it. As for "the spiritual," that includes all the planes of consciousness above the ordinary mind. It is the way of ascent. And that is where I repeatedly and emphatically, and from experience, say that those great Experiences, which have to be turned into spiritual summits, are part of the mental bubble (including the overmind): they are the rarefied summits on which the being thins out into a marvelous whiteness, immense, royal, without a ripple of trouble, in an eternal peace—which can last for millenniums without its changing the world one iota, by definition. But the spiritual is not the supramental, and when one touches the supramental, it seems to be almost a whole other Spirit, it is so compact, warm, powerful, present, embodied and radiantly solid in broad daylight. That is the Radiance which Sri Aurobindo and Mother came to bring down on earth—they said over and over that their yoga was new, new, new—and it is through the simple little fire inside us that we can enter into direct contact with That, without sitting in the lotus position or leaving life. When one touches That, the "spiritual" heights seem pale. That is all I have to say. So we do not at all need to be super-yogis to have this contact, and those who have found Nirvana, or what have you, have not advanced one inch toward That, because the clue to That is not up there at all or outside, but in your own small capacity of flame.

So, if instead of splitting hairs, you set out boldly on the road, afire, you would perhaps discover that we are indeed at the Hour of God and that a single spark of sincere effort, at one's own level, opens doors which have been closed for millenniums.

Satprem

P.S. To help you read Mother, I am enclosing two texts by her.
"One could say that it is far more difficult to go from the mental to the supramental life than to go from a certain psychic emotion in life—something that is like a reflection, a luminous emanation of the divine Presence in matter—to the supramental consciousness; it is much easier to go from that into the supramental consciousness than to go from the highest intellectual speculation to any supramental vibration. Perhaps it is the word that misleads us! Perhaps it is because we call it 'supramental' that we expect to reach it through a higher intellectual mental activity. But the reality is quite different. With this very high and pure and lofty intellectual activity, one seems

to go towards a kind of cold, powerless abstraction, an icy light that is surely very remote from life and still further away from the experience of the supramental reality.

"The new substances that is spreading and acting in the world contains a warmth, a power, a joy so intense that all intellectual activity seems cold and dry beside it. And that is why the less one talks about these things, the better it is. A single instant, a single impulse of deep and true love, a single minute of deep communion with the divine Grace brings you much closer to the goal than all possible explanations."

(Questions and Answers, 5.14.1958)

Whatever we see of this Divine and fix our concentrated effort on it, that we can become or grow into some kind of unity with it or at the lowest into tune and harmony with it.... Whatever of it we see, we can create or reveal in our conscious nature and being and can grow into it. . ..

Sri Aurobindo

The Mother, The Spiritual Significance of Flowers,
Part 1, pp. 59-60

Morwenna Donnelly

The secret of the right attitude to take in difficulty is contained in Sri Aurobindo's description of his system of spiritual practice as 'a sunlit way'. It is the secret of an absolute trust in the Divine; of a quiet and happy confidence and faith in the aspirant's own divine potentialities, whatever obstacles lie in the course of their unfoldment; and of a steady affirmation of all that the positive way enjoins.

In order to understand this better, let us look for a moment at some of the things Sri Aurobindo has written about the distinctive characteristics of the sunlit path and the qualities which it requires in those who chose it. As we have already seen, Sri Aurobindo, though he does not in any way condemn the negative means for those who wish to get away from life, states that they are disadvantageous from the positive point of view and the attempt to transform life. In another context, defining the negative and positive means of removing difficulties, he explains: "By negative I mean merely repressing the desires and wrong movements and egoism, by positive mean the bringing down of light and peace and purity in those parts from above. I do not mean that these movements are not to be rejected - but all the energy should not be used solely for rejection. It must also be directed to the positive replacement of them by the higher consciousness. The more this consciousness comes, the easier also will the rejection be."

In another place, speaking of the practice of vairagya (turning away from life), he admits its occasional utility as a counterbalance to a too strong vital pull, but says that it tends, through a tamasic element of despair and depression, to "dilapidate the fire of the being and may lead in some cases to falling between two stools so that one loses earth and misses heaven".

He therefore prefers to replace vairagya by a quiet, resolute rejection of wrong movements. This rejection does not include the destruction of any of those activities and powers, such as painting, music, poetry, which can be made instruments of the Yoga and the divine work, but these must find a new and spiritual base. "Yoga can be done without the rejection of life," he writes, "without killing or impairing the life-joy or the vital force." Any inclination to deny life or the world and disappear into the Indefinable he objects to as being incompatible with this Yoga, with its aim of bringing the Divine into life.

There are certain conditions necessary for following the sunlit path, principally that the psychic being is constantly or usually in front, or that there is a natural spirit of surrender and faith or a face turned habitually to the sun. If the psychic being is strong and master of the being there is little or no subjective suffering. Instead "the way is sunlit and a great joy and sweetness are the note of the whole sadhana".

Sri Aurobindo teaches that true vision rises above what he calls the "intellectual-ethical virtue-and-sin dodge which is only a mental construction of practical value for the outward life but not a truth of inner values" and sees only harmonies and disharmonies which must be set right. Obstacles, he says, "have to be looked at as something wrong in the machinery of human nature which has to be changed - they should not be regarded as sins or wrongdoings which make one despair of oneself and the sadhana".

A seeing of ourselves and of all the complex forces that move on the stage of our being, not from any dry outer intellectual or

ethical viewpoint, but from an inner spiritual observation, "a living perception of how things are done in us", can be intensely interesting and bring "a living mastery over this inner universe".

Wonderful indeed would be the aspirant who could escape, in the early stages of the sadhana, some periods in which he did not feel like a fly caught helplessly in the intricate web woven about him by his nature; nevertheless the habit of dispassion, urged by Sri Aurobindo, of quiet and detached interest in all the arduous and yet marvelous task of transformation which the Divine Master initiates in every being he calls to Yoga, can be the staunchest of supports in the sadhana.

The artist, struggling to create, possesses this power to be steadfastly centred in the processes of his task and to feel an absorbed interest even when the material seems to rebel, knowing that each solution found to the problems of his art brings him nearer greater mastery, and this is the attitude to the difficulties of Yoga which every sadhaka should possess.

Those aspirants who allow their faults or failures to depress or discourage them unduly, only make the way rougher. "It does not matter what defects you may have in your nature," Sri Aurobindo says encouragingly. "The one thing that matters is keeping yourself open to the Force. Nobody can transform himself by his own unaided efforts; it is only the Divine Force that can transform him. If you keep yourself open, all the rest will be done for you."

Despondency and shame, ideas of incapacity and a dwelling on defects are weakening things. One should not always be thinking of defects and wrong movements but concentrate primarily on what one is trying to be. "Turn your eyes more to the coming light," he tells a disciple, "and less to any immediate darkness." To be constantly observing faults and failures causes depression and discourages the faith.

In another place he writes: "Free yourself from all exaggerated self-depreciation and the habit of getting depressed by the sense of sin, difficulty or failure. These feelings do not really help; on the contrary, they are an immense obstacle and hamper the progress. They belong to the religious, not to the Yogic mentality." The sadhaka must look on all defects as movements of the lower nature, common to all, and reject them, "calmly, firmly and persistently with full confidence in the Divine Power - without weakness or depression or negligence and without excitement, impatience or violence".

Too continual an emphasis on the dark side of things only increases the force of the difficulties. "It is a subtle law of the action of consciousness that if you stress difficulties you have to observe them, of course, but not stress them, they will quite sufficiently do that for themselves the difficulties tend to stick or even increase; On the contrary if you put your whole stress on faith and aspiration and concentrate steadily on what you aspire to, that will sooner or later tend towards realization." This mood of affirmation was well stressed in the injunction: Whatsoever things ye desire when ye pray, believe that ye have received them and ye shall have them.

Always fight out the difficulty at once, says Sri Aurobindo, and hold on resolutely to the idea that, taken in the right attitude, adversity becomes an opportunity for advance. And the only right attitude is to become always more quiet, firmer in the will to go through to the end; to open more and more effectually to the Light; to continue to make "an affirmation of faith even in the midst of obscurity, faith in the presence of a Power that is working behind the cloud and the veil, in the guidance of the Guru, by an observation of oneself to find any cause of the arrest, not in a spirit of depression or discouragement but with the will to find out and remove it."

A quiet, steady rejection of defects, made in absolute sincerity (the sine qua non of the Yoga) will finally cast them out, for, as Sri Aurobindo observes, each victory means new strength for further victories.

To indulge a desire or false movement will often give a worse recoil in the sadhana than to disappoint it, and in the later stages to give in over a small point may mean losing a whole battle, so important do even minor details become. If the vital or mental being are exposed to disturbing touches, the answer is to live more deeply within, for the inmost psychic being "is not oppressed by them; it stands in its own closeness to the Divine and sees the small surface movements as surface things foreign to the true Being".

There are always difficulties in the beginning for all aspirants; even for the advanced, the Vedic sages tell us, there are still problems: "As one ascends from peak to peak, there is made clear the much that has still to be done." Therefore in the beginning of your practice, Sri Aurobindo says, be patient; a slow development is the best anyone can hope for in the first years. Cherish the small beginnings. The Yogin knows "that the neutral quiet so dissatisfying to the vital eagerness of the sadhaka is the first step towards the peace that passeth all understanding, the small current or thrill of inner delight the first trickling of the ocean of Ananda, the play of lights or colours, the key of the doors of the inner vision and experience, the descent that stiffens the body into a concentrated stillness the first touch of something at the end of which is the presence of the Divine. He is not impatient; he is rather careful not to disturb the evolution that is beginning." Moderation, he cautions, is needed even in the eagerness for progress. "People who are cheerful and ready to go even slowly step by step, march faster and more securely than those who are impatient and in haste."

Depression is a negative thing, like fear, and belongs to the vital. It is "a clouded grey state" which obstructs the inner light and increases difficulty, and he quotes the injunction of the Gita: "Yoga should be practiced persistently with a heart free from depression."

A constant recurrence of despair, despondency, doubt and revolt are often due to mental or vital formations which seize the vital mind at the slightest excuse and make it revolve in the same well-worn circle, in the same mechanical way that the body responds to the habit of illness. Make the vital mind once withdraw its consent from these habitual movements and refuse to believe in the suggestions or feelings that start them and they will cease. A firm pressure of expulsion is always a better way to deal with resistances or hostile suggestions than to struggle with them, for all reactions that disturb the quietude and cover up the inner being, mitigate against an easy outcome. The most important thing is to become quieter and quieter, Sri Aurobindo says; to look on an adverse influence as something which has intruded; to separate yourself from it, deny it, and abide in a quiet confidence in the Divine Power.

This quiet confidence is to be distinguished from self-assurance, as true humility is to be distinguished from that self-depreciation that expresses itself in an ostentatious parade of being sinful, which is the negative inversion of spiritual pride.

Nevertheless, because Sri Aurobindo always comes down firmly on the use of the positive qualities in the sadhana, he maintains that an excessive optimism is better and more helpful in sadhana than an excessive pessimism.

This does not mean sailing blithely along without noticing one's faults. To recognize wrong movements of idea, feeling, speech or action is the first condition of inner progress. It means learning that equanimity which is not touched or troubled by anything said or done to one, seeing them "with a straight look, free from the distortions created by personal feeling, and to try to understand what is behind them, why they happen, what is to be learnt from them, what is it in oneself which they are cast against and what inner profit or progress one can make out of them; it means self-mastery over the vital movements anger and sensitiveness and pride as well as desire and the rest - not to let them get hold of the emotional being and disturb the inner peace, not to speak and act in the rush and impulsion of these things, always to act and speak out of a calm inner poise of the spirit .... Equality means another thing - to have an equal view of men and their nature and acts and the forces that move them; it helps one to see truth about them by pushing away from the mind all personal feelings in one's seeing and judgement and even all the mental bias." This equanimity is certainly not easy, but one should always try to make it increasingly the basis of one's inner state and outer movements.

Just as there are forces concerned to depress and discourage, so there are also forces to restore and strengthen, and the aspirant must develop the power to draw upon these resources. Once something of the Truth has shown within "it will always, even if for a time heavily clouded over with wrong movements, shine out again like the sun in heaven. Therefore persevere with confidence and never lose courage."

There is strength even in the weakest. No formation of strength or weakness is final; at any moment it may change, and does so change, we are told, particularly under the pressure of Yoga, where at any moment there may be seen "weakness changing into power, the incapable becoming capable, suddenly or slowly the instrumental consciousness rising to a new stature or developing its latent powers". Spiritual endeavour does not depend for its success on the determined will of the aspirant; it depends on a combination of his will with the help given by the Divine Power.

Dryness in Yoga can be greatly reduced, as has been stressed already, if the sadhaka has what Sri Aurobindo calls an ardour of introspection and self-conquest and finds every step of the effort and struggle interesting. It is also reduced if the aspirant can once achieve that trust which feels the hand of the Divine in each turn of the path, and the grace and guidance even in difficulty, but at the same time does not always demand or expect to understand its workings.

The secret of weathering the ordeals of the path, as in so much else in the Yoga, lies in the heart, not in the mind, though the mind, by holding firmly to the truth in attacks, can by its alliance greatly assist, especially in those stages before the psychic being has fully come forward. If the psychic being is to the fore, difficulties are not felt as definitive but as imperfections which the Grace will remove: once the heart can open its inner doors "the soul looks out in a blaze of trust and self-giving. Before that fire the debates of the mind and its difficulties wither away and the path however long or arduous becomes a sunlit road not only towards but through love and Ananda."

Few can attain such rightfulness of spirit at first, but patient constancy will win it. "Grumble," says Sri Aurobindo to a disciple in difficulties, "if your nature compels you to it, but persevere," and his final word to all those experiencing trouble is contained in the simple instruction: "Be faithful and you will conquer."

Founding the Life Divine, The Right Attitude in Difficulty, Morwenna Donnelly, pp.134-143

What do you want the Yoga for? To get power? To attain to peace and calm? To serve humanity?

None of these motives is sufficient to show that you are meant for the Path.

The question you are to answer is this: Do you want the Yoga for the sake of the Divine? Is the Divine the supreme fact of your life, so much so that it is simply impossible for you to do without it? Do you feel that your very raison d'être is the Divine and without it there is no meaning in your existence? If so, then only can it be said that you have a call for the path.

The Mother
The Mother, The Spiritual Significance of Flowers,
Part 1, p. 61

ALAIN GRANDCOLAS

A pioneer Aurovilian Alain Grandcolas wrote to us (B and Franz) that the Mother changed her mind about advocating the sunlit path due to her physical suffering at the end of her life. Alain quotes from *Mother's Agenda* to substantiate his speculation. While we are not in agreement with his conclusions, it is perhaps useful to share his position in order to clarify further our understanding of what the sunlit path really is. We understand that the sunlit path is not a denial of pain and difficulty; rather it is an affirmation that light prevails over darkness, wisdom over ignorance, and immortality over death as the Vedas have always taught. To realize and live that is the sunlit path of Integral Yoga.

Alain writes:
"What the Mother told to Satprem in 1961 in Her dream to carve a Sunlit Path for everybody is often quoted and very appealing:

"There is always (it is probable inevitable) the path of struggle and then there is the Sunlit Path.

And after much study and investigation, I have had a sort of spiritual ambition, if it may be called that, to bring to the world a Sunlit Path in order to eliminate the need for suffering and struggle..."[8].

Later on, considering her own experiences in her body and in her consciousness from January 1971 onwards, The Mother changed Her views: the path she is carving implies a very demanding sadhana with much unbearable suffering.

---
8. The Mother, Agenda, Vol. 2, p. 260 (30.9.1961)

On 18.9.1971, the Mother gives the following indication, maybe the first one on the subject. She passes *"from the most dreadful uneasiness... to a marvel. It is strange. An unutterable bliss"*[9]. Up to now, many of us are considering uneasiness as the outcome of not following the tiny indication from the psychic being. It is an alarming feeling, extremely useful, which is meant to draw the attention and invites to redirect the attitude and to reconsider the thinking.

In 1972, it seems that the Mother is developing doubts on this Sunlit Path She wanted to create for Her disciples. On that year, it happened that important uneasiness and psychological unbearable sufferings rose from the subconscient, Her own subconcient as well as the subconscient of the "others" and the subconscient of the earth.

In 7 April 1973, one and half month before stopping to share with Satprem the evolution of Her sadhana, She told to him: *"I seem to be gathering all the world's resistances.... They come to me one after another, and if I weren't.... If I stop calling the Divine for a single minute, intimately feeling his presence within me, the pain is unbearable, mon petit! To such a point that I now hesitate to speak of "transformation" to people, because if that's what it is, one really has to be a hero.... You see, there's something in the body that would almost howl nonstop."*[10]

Some days later, on 25 April 1973 (p. 410) the Mother confirms: *"it's more than difficult.... I am sorry, I thought I was suffering for everybody – but I see it isn't the case."* [11]

---

9 The Mother, Agenda, Vol. 12, p. 160 (18.9.1971).
10 The Mother, Agenda, Vol. 13, p. 260 (7.4.1973).
11 The Mother, Agenda, Vol. 13, p. 265p; (25.4.1973).

In other words, Her disciples on this path have to meet unbearable tribulations.

And the last mention of this suffering is on the 14 May 1973, five days before stopping relating Her sadhana: *All the time I have to keep a grip on myself not to howl.... From time to time, there's a marvelous moment – but it's short!"*[12]

What happened between that 14 May and the 17 November 1973, when the Mother left Her Body, is not known. There is nothing to give a hint that She may have changed Her views.

We are allowed to be perplexed. We now remember the epitaph which the Mother has written for the Sri Aurobindo's samadhi: " *Thee who has suffered so much...*" We cannot help from linking this suffering with the second preoccupation of Sri Aurobindo. His last known utterance was dictated in 1947:"*My present effort is to bring "something" of the Supermind down here..... but at the present stage, the progressive supramentalisation of the overmind is the first immediate preoccupation and the second is the lightening of the heavy resistance of the Inconscient...*"

The path towards supermanhood which has been carved by the Mother is only for people who have the qualities and the determination to live in a heroic manner. Happen what may."

---

12 The Mother, Agenda, Vol. 13, p. 271 (14.5.1973).

Maggi Lidchi Grassi

Once, when asked the secret of her spiritual growth, Maggie Lidchi Grassi, a secretary of the Mother, responded, *"I take everything, good and bad, as a Blessing and a Grace from The Mother"*—a yogic attitude described as *"the Sunlit Path"* in Sri Aurobindo's yoga.

Children of Change, by Amrit, p. 469

When you come to the Yoga, you must be ready to have all your mental buildings and all your vital scaffoldings shattered to pieces. You must be prepared to be suspended in the air with nothing to support you except your faith. You will have to forget your past self and its clingings altogether, to pluck it out of your consciousness and be born anew, free from every kind of bondage. Think not of what you were, but of what you aspire to be; be altogether in what you want to realise. Turn from your dead past and look straight towards the future.

The Mother

The Mother, The Spiritual Significance of Flowers,
Part 1, p. 61

Nolini Kanta Gupta

The devastation and horror of World War II might seem to overshadow the idea of a Sunlit Path. Nolini Kanta Gupta, sadhak, scholar and former trustee of the Sri Aurobindo Ashram has written in *The Advent* (February 1970) quoting a past editorial from 1945 (page 40). He extends the sunlit path beyond the individual to the nation. Now in the time of a global pandemic, we would extend it to the world.

Sri Aurobindo speaks of the sunlit path in Yoga. It is the path of happy progress where dangers and difficulties, violent ups and downs are reduced to a minimum, if not altogether obviated. In ideal conditions it is as it were a smooth and fair-weather sailing, as much of course as it is humanly possible. What are then these conditions? It is when the sadhaka keeps touch with his inmost being, his psychic consciousness, when this inner Guide and Helmsman is given the charge; for then he will be able to pass sovereignly by all shoals and rocks and storm-racks, through all vicissitudes gliding on—slow or swift as needed:—inevitably towards the goal. A doubting mind, an impetuous vital urge, an inert physical consciousness, though they may be there in any strength, cannot disturb or upset the even tenor of the forward march. Even outward circumstances bow down to the pressure of the psychic temperament and bring to' it their happy collaboration.

This may not always mean that all is easy and difficulty is simply not, once the psychic is there. It becomes so when the psychic is there fully in front, even otherwise when the inner being is in the background, still sensed and, on the whole, obeyed, although there are battles, hard battles to be fought and won, then even a little of this Consciousness saves from a great fear. For then, in all circumstances you will have found a secret joy and cheer and strength that buoy you up and carry you through.

Like the individual, nations too have their sunlit path and the path of the doldrum as well. So long as a nation keeps to the truth of its inner being, follows its natural line of development, remains faithful to its secret godhead, it will have chosen that good part which will bring it divine blessings and fulfilment. But sometimes a nation has the stupidity to deny its self, to run after a ignis fatuus, a māyāmrga, then grief and sorrow and frustration lie ahead. We are afraid India did take such a wrong step when she refused to see the great purpose behind the present war and tried to avoid contributing her mite to the evolutionary Force at work. On the other hand, Britain, in a moment of supreme crisis, that meant literally life or death, not only to herself or to other nations, but to humanity itself, had the good fortune to be led by the right Inspiration, the whole nation rose as one man and swore allegiance to the cause of humanity and the gods. That was how she was saved and that was how she aquired a new merit and a fresh lease of life. Unlike Britain, France bowed down and accepted what should not have been accepted and cut herself adrift from its inner life and truth, the result was five years of hell. Fortunately, the hell, in the end, proved to be a purgatory, but what a purgatory! For there were souls who were willing to pay the price and did pay it to the full cash and net. So France has been given the chance again to turn round and take up the thread of its life where it snapped. . .

If the present war has any meaning, as we all declare it has, then we must never lose sight of that meaning. And our true victory will come only in the process of the realisation of that meaning. That is the sunlit path we refer to here which the nations have to follow in their mutual dealings. It is the path of the evolutionary call to which we say we have responded and to which we must remain loyal and faithful in thought, in speech and in deed. If we see dark and ominous clouds gathering round us, dangers and difficulties suddenly raising their heads, then we must look about and try honestly to find out whether we have not strayed away from the sunlit path.

Nagin Doshi Questioned Sri Aurobindo about the Sunlit Path

Nagin: After passing through a lot of attacks, falls, depressions, some part of my inmost being seems to have a fleeting glimpse of what is called the sunlit or golden path. Once on this road no hostile being can touch the inner being. Darkness or ignorance (unwillingness to change) is worked out in the part itself without the necessity (as is normal) of its rising up and veiling the elevated or illumined parts of the being.

Revolts, doubts or even suggestions fail to break the luminous environment of this pilgrim. Not that these anti-divine things do not attempt to approach him. They do pursue him a long way. But he only looks at them, smiles and journeys on. To keep up with the sunlit path requires a watchful eye and one-pointed concentration, which does not heed what lies on the side-tracks. His soul secretly companions him throughout with its peace, joy and love. Does such a path truly exist somewhere or is it only a visionary idea?

Sri Aurobindo: There is such a sunlit or golden path, but it is difficult for man with the pull of his lower nature to follow it.

Nagin: Difficult no doubt it is, but is it really impossible for the human being to tread the sunlit path?

Sri Aurobindo: It is not impossible. But only one or two have been able to do it — which proves that it is not easy.

Nagin: Can't one do something for a smooth transformation of one's external nature with no serious revolts, attacks or falls?

Sri Aurobindo: Yes. but it is not easy. It needs either a calm resolute will governing the whole being or a very great samata to have a quite smooth transformation. If they are there, then there are no revolts though there may be difficulties, no attacks, only a conscious dealing with the defects of the nature, no falls but only setting right of wrong steps or movements.

Nagin: About some sadhaks who do not need to pass through the struggle of the sadhana, you said, "It is something in their nature that is poised, calm, open." Do you think there is anything like that in my nature?

Sri Aurobindo: There is a possibility of it, it is an element, but there was also too much tamas for it to dominate the whole nature.

Nagin: Before I came down into the physical from the higher consciousness, I had the belief that I could remain always on the sunlit path. Was it wrong?

Sri Aurobindo: It was not wrong but a part of your being, the tamasic part has not allowed you to realise it all through. You have what many people here lack, a capacity of poise or balance. It is again the inertia that allows the vital attacks to dash against it and create a suggestion of revolt — for with the perfect balance any tendency to revolt is impossible.

Nagin: Since my being wants the sunlit path, kindly enlighten me how to make it possible.

Sri Aurobindo: It is possible if you (1) can get free of the vital demand, (2) regard the difficulties of the nature calmly and dispassionately as if some defects of a machine that has to be set right, the being that uses the machine remaining fully dedicated to the Mother.

Nagin Doshi, *Guidance from Sri Aurobindo*, Vol. II p.155

Narendra Thakkar

"The Divine Mother's Divinity is infinite and indescribable in human terms. The human mind cannot grasp it, not understand it, not judge it. But ever a little of Her Divinity is enough to uplift and illumine the human soul into a realm of Light. Sri Aurobindo in his book The Mother *talks of the threefold effort: Aspiration, Rejection and Surrender. By this the Sunlit Path can be found and followed.*"

Booklet The Glory of Darshan (2017)

Vikas (Alan Vickers)

British architect Alan Vikers is a pioneer Aurovilian known as "Vikas" who described his journey as:

. . . a work still very much in progress after more than 48 years, but by following Sri Aurobindo's 'Integral Yoga' I definitely feel that I am somewhere in the foothills. And rather than make a wretched battle out of the process, I have aspired to walk what Mother called 'the sunlit path', which requires a surrender to the inner guide, who, one anyway discovers, has been leading us even when we thought we were doing the yoga.

Connect (Journal of Auroville International USA). Winter 2019/2020

NARAD

Narad (Richard Eggenberger) is a pioneer of Auroville given the work of the Gardens of Matrimandir by the Mother.

The Clear and Sunlit Way

A longing that constrains the breath,
Hopes that will not die,
A certitude outlasting death
And life's indignity.
A dream of unpolluted earth,
The blue of crystal skies,
A crucible for higher birth
And heaven's majesties.
Descend once more O stainless feet,
Touch our sacred soil,
Cleanse our hearts of all deceit
That we may knowing toil
To hasten the advent of the day
The centuries have sought,
Walk now the clear and sunlit way
Transcending mortal thought.

From *Poems by Narad*. 2004.

Kireet Joshi

Dr. Kireet Joshi, an eminent sadhak and scholar, in his explication of the Isha Upanishad establishes our destination in a sunlit path:

One not only sees the Self or God, one even embraces Him and become that Reality. The Isha Upanishad describes the great experience culminating in identity in the following terms:

But he who sees everywhere the Self in all existences and all existences in the Self, shrinks not thereafter from anything. He in whom it is the Self-being that has become all existences that are Becomings, for he has the perfect knowledge, how shall he be deluded, whence shall he have grief who sees everywhere oneness? (Isha Upanishad, 6,7.)

With this culmination in identity, one is able to live in the supreme Vedantic knowledge, "He am I"

Such is the foundational knowledge that Yoga promises, and from this foundational knowledge, several practical capacities of knowledge and will can be developed which should lift us from what Sri Aurobindo calls seven-fold ignorance to seven-fold integral knowledge. The result for practical life would be elimination of ignorance in our thought will, sensations, actions, and prevention from returning wrong or imperfect responses to the questionings of the world, liberation from wandering in a maze of errors and desires, strivings and failures, pain and pleasure, sin and stumbling. Our crooked road of blind groping and changing goal is turned into a sunlit path.[13]

---

13 Yoga of Sri Aurobindo and other Essays, p.259

Dr. Joshi summarizes the journey to the sunlit path in Sri Aurobindo's Yoga:

According to Sri Aurobindo, there is in the human being a psychic entity or the divine individual soul. This soul puts forward a formation, which evolves gradually in the human complex of the body, life and mind. It is that formation which is called the psychic being. This psychic being is constantly at work in order to awaken the body, life and mind, so that by that awakening, these instruments (body, life and mind) turn to the higher realities and the Supreme Divine, who is the ultimate origin of all that is in the universe. The psychic being also acts as a guide and a teacher of these instruments, but like all good teachers, it does not impose itself on these instruments. It acts more through influence, suggestions and counsels, which are heard as it were in the deeper recesses of the heart. The psychic being inspires body, life and mind to give their consent for their awakening and their turning to the divine consciousness. This consent, when obtained, is a necessary condition for a rapid growth of these instruments. The more decisive is the consent, the greater is the efficacy of the psychic being. As a result, the psychic being becomes more and more powerful, and ultimately it floods its light on the instruments and makes these instruments more and more trained, more and more perfect and suffused with the psychic light.

This process is, in the beginning quite slow, and therefore, the psychic being, lives in the body, life and mind as some-thing not quite fully grown up. Human life is a process by which, through varieties of experiences, it teaches us that we need to awaken to the presence of the psychic being, who is secretly sitting in the deep cave of the heart. That is why, the great teachers of mankind have counseled us to, look deeper and deeper in the heart and enter into a long tunnel at the end of which one can discover that deepest psychic being. Once we can reach that psychic being, we can get true guidance more and more readily, and we can walk on the path of life as on a sunlit path.

Nachiketas / A Synoptic Essay on Immortality p. 76-7

Rosemary Meran

Rosemary Meran is originally from the Dominican Republic but has lived in various parts of the world including Auroville. B discovered in one of her poems this intuitive grasp of the sunlit path. This is an excerpt:

> *. . . In front of me there was a path*
> *illuminated, wide*
> *bounded by silence and peace*
> *the ground covered with fallen golden roble flowers*
> *it seemed like a solitary trail*
> *with tall flowering trees welcoming*
> *the unassuming wisdom guiding my steps*
> *As I studied this path further*
> *noticing how the sunlight played*
> *with the shadows of the trees*
> *a familiar feeling began to well up*
> *rivulets of pinks and whites and golds*
> *down the crown of my head and into my heart*
> *the beauty of the inner vision engulfing my senses*
> *I remained steady, unmoving, still*
> *drawn to the mystery of swirling colours*
> *traveling from the base of my spine*
> *and into the centre of my being*
> *enlivening every space*
> *pulsating light rushing through*
> *Meanwhile, on the surface, a voice*
> *unsettled and unimpressed by the passage of time*
> *wanting to reach the depth of the nameless*

needing to touch the concealed luminescence
of no-thingness before the imminent birth of the All
A secret flame slowly awakening
quietly spiraling, a beingness
emerging from a rayless void
ready to build its home in my Spirit
its life kindled by the unknown
dripping down into my body drop by drop
softening my edges
blessing me with its presence
all encompassing, complete
giving way to a moment of recognition
My heart ablaze
stubborn in its desire
to live within the hands of the eternal
surrendering deeper
offering what I have of myself
In a moment's breath
existence became the music . . . .

When B communicated with Rose about her poem, he sent her some sunlit path quotations. She replied with another poem. Here is part of it:

On this new path
the stones become like friends
a sacred journey home
where time breaks free
. . .
To live from joy

I am here

To Love beyond the known
i am here

To soar within the inner landscapes of my soul and yours
I am here

To taste the laughter of the ineffable
and bring about the rapture of His spirit into my flesh
I am here

To breathe easy as i swim in a golden sea of truth
I am here

To know and live in beauty and grace and the music of the stars
I am here

To witness you and me as the very Self
I am here

Mind and body expanding
Light endless Light
the only reality

"... The Happy Sunlit Path"

Remember, My child, I am always with you, deep in your soul,
At all hours remember, I watch over your life and progress,
With love and care and guide your uncertain steps.
Remember me wherever you may be in the world.
Repeat my name whenever you have a little time to spare,
I am present everywhere. To see and feel my presence, my child,
You have only to switch on the Inner Light.
I am inside you, outside you, above and below.
You can feel my love with only a little warmth on your side.
Remember, I never abandon you even
                         when you go out of the happy sunlit path.
Remember my love always, I never scold or punish, that is not my way.
I am pouring my love in your heart day and night.
Remember, I am your Mother, Father, counselor and Queen.
Remember me always for I am your closest, faithful
                                   and dearest friend.
Hide nothing from me. Depend on me for all your needs.
Remember you are my child, I can never be ashamed of you,
Whatever you do, remember me, I shall give you sunshine,
Laughter and joy in life which no one can take away from you.
In spite of your thousand mistakes, hold on to me, remember,
                                   my child can never fail.
Tell me all your thousand mistakes, hold on to me, remember,
                                   my child can never fail.
Tell me all your plans and dreams. I am always with you.
Remember, I love and protect you.
Remember me when afraid, no one can do any harm to you.
I want you to be really good, always happy my child.

Remember, I live in the heart of all living beings,
                                        human and animal.
When you are kind to anyone, remember you are kind to me.
Be generous as the ocean, fill the world with good thoughts
                                        and feelings.
Be straight and simple, remember me always without fail.
Enter your heart to know what I like, remember never to tell a lie.
I shall put within your reach all that is noble and beautiful.
Have the utmost goodwill for all, remember all are my children.
Remember me for any help for I am always with you day and night.
Remember, my child, your life is worth living only
                                        in the service of the divine.

                                        The Mother

Epilogue

"The Way of the Sunlit Path"

is a gift of guidance and love from

Sri Aurobindo and the Mother.

Now, we journey home on this Sunlit Path

experiencing that joy—seeing it, feeling it.

The Sunlit Path echos in this mantra from Savitri:

By Light we live and to the Light we go . . .

International Publications

Auroville Architecture
by Franz Fassbender

Auroville Form Style and Design
by Franz Fassbender

Landscapes and Gardens of Auroville
by Franz Fassbender

Inauguration of Auroville
by Franz Fassbender

Auroville in a Nutshell
by Tim Wrey

Death doesn't exist
The Mother on Death, Sri Aurobindo on Rebirth
Compiled by Franz Fassbender

Divine Love
Compiled by Franz Fassbender

Five Dream
by Sri Aurobindo

A Vision
Compiled by Franz Fassbender

Passage to More than India
by Dick Batstone

The Mother on Japan
Compiled by Franz Fassbender

Children of Change: A Spiritual Pilgrimage
by Amrit (Howard Shoji Iriyama)

Memories of Auroville - told by early Aurovilians
by Janet Feran

The Journeying Years
by Dianna Bowler

Auroville Reflected
by Bindu Mohanty

Finding the Psychic Being
by Loretta Shartsis

The Teachings of Flowers
The Life and Work of the Mother of the Sri Aurobindo Ashram
by Loretta Shartsis

The Supramental Transformation
by Loretta Shartsis

**The Mother's Yoga - 1956-1973 (English & French)
Vol. 1, 1956-1967 & Vol. 2, 1968-1973**
by Loretta Shartsis

Antithesis of Yoga
by Jocelyn Janaka

Bougainvilleas PROTECTION
by Narad (Richard Eggenberger), Nilisha Mehta

Crossroad The New Humanity
by Paulette Hadnagy

Die Praxis Des Integralen Yoga
by M. P. Pandit

The Way of the Sunlit Path
by William Sullivan

Wildlife great and small of India's Coromandel
by Tim Wrey

A New Education With A Soul
by Marguerite Smithwhite

Featured Titles

Divine Love

The texts presented in this book are selected from the Mother and Sri Aurobindo.

"Awakened to the meaning of my heart. That to feel love and oneness is to live. And this the magic of our golden change, is all the truth I know or seek, O sage."

Sri Aurobindo, Savitri, Book XII, Epilog

A Vision by the Mother

On 28th May 1958, the Mother recounted a vision she once had of a wonderful Being of Love and Consciousness, emanated from the Supreme Origin and projected directly into the Inconscient so that the creation would gradually awaken to the Supramental Consciousness. The Mother's account of this vision was brought out a first time in November 1906, in the Revue Cosmique, a monthly review published in Paris.

A Dream – Aims and Ideals of Auroville
the Mother on Auroville

50 years of Auroville from 28.02.1968 - 28.02.2018

Today, information about Auroville is abundant. Many people try to make meaning out of Auroville – about its conception, to what direction should we grow towards, and, what are we doing here?

But what was Mother's original Dream and what was her Vision for Auroville back then?

Matrimandir Talks by the Mother

This book presents most of Mother's Matrimandir talks, including how she conceived the idea for this special concentration and meditation building in Auroville.

Memories of Auroville - Told by early Aurovilians

Memories of Auroville is a book about the very early days of Auroville based on interviews made in 1997 with Aurovilians who lived here between 1968 and 1973. The interviews presented in this book are part of a history program for newcomers that I had created with my friend, Philip Melville in 1997. The plan was to divide Auroville's history into different eras and then interview Aurovilians according to their area of knowledge.

Our first section would cover the years from 1968 till 1973 when the Mother was still in her physical body.

The Way of the Sunlit Path

May The Way of the Sunlit Path be a convenient guide for activating this ancient truth as a support for a Conscious Evolution.

May it illumine the transformation offered to us in the Integral Yoga.

A Dream Takes Shape (in English, French, Hindi)

A comprehensive brochure on the international township of Auroville in, ranging from its Charter and "Why Auroville?" to the plan of the township, the central Matrimandir, the national pavilions and residences, to working groups, the economy, making visits, how to join, its relationship to the Sri Aurobindo Ashram, and its key role in the future of the world. This brochure endeavours to highlight how The Mother envisioned Auroville from its inception, some of the major achievements realised over the years, and some of the difficulties currently faced in implementing the guidelines which she gave.

Mother on Japan

I had everything to learn in Japan. For four years, from an artistic point of view, I lived from wonder to wonder. And everything in this city, in this country, from beginning to end, gives you the impression of impermanence, of the unexpected, the exceptional... ...everything in this city, in this country, from beginning to end, gives you the impression of impermanence, of the unexpected, the exceptional. You always come to things you did not expect; you want to find them again and they are lost – they have made something else which is equally charming.

Auroville Reflected

On 28 February 1968, on an impoverished plateau on the Coromandel Coast of South India, about 4,000 people from around the world gathered for a most unusual inauguration. Handfuls of soil from the countries of the world were mixed together as a symbol of human unity. Why did Indira Gandhi, the erstwhile Prime Minister of India, support this development for "a city the earth needs?" Why did UNESCO endorse this project? Why does the Dalai Lama continue to be involved in the project? What led anthropologist Margaret Mead to insist that records must be kept of its progress? Why did both historian William Irwin Thompson and United Nations representative Robert Muller note that this social experiment may be a breakthrough for humanity even as critics commented, "it is an impossible dream"?

A House For the Third Millennium
Essays on Matrimandir

Nightwatch at the Matrimandir...
A cosmic spectacle; the black expanse above, the big black crater of Matrimandir's excavation carved deep into the soil. The four pillars - two of which are completed and the other two nearing completion - are four huge ships coming together from the four corners of the earth to meet at this pro propitious spot...

Passage to More than India

This book is a voyage of discovery. In 1959 the author, Dick Batstone, a classically educated bookseller in England, with a Christian background, comes across a life of the great Indian polymath Sri Aurobindo, though a series of apparently fortuitous circumstances. A meeting in Durham, England, leads him to a determination to get to the Sri Aurobindo Ashram in Pondicherry, a former French territory south of Madras.

www.ingramcontent.com/pod-product-compliance
Lightning Source LLC
LaVergne TN
LVHW010427070526
838199LV00066B/5951